THE TWELVE DISCIPLES

DOUGLAS CONNELLY

10 STUDIES
FOR INDIVIDUALS
OR GROUPS

Life
Builder
Study

INTER-VARSITY PRESS
36 Causton Street, London SW1P 4ST, England
Email: ivp@ivpbooks.com
Website: www.ivpbooks.com

Originally published in the United States of America in the LifeGuide® Bible Studies series
in 1992 by InterVarsity Press, Downers Grove, Illinois
First published in Great Britain by Scripture Union in 2014
This edition published in Great Britain by Inter-Varsity Press 2018

British Library Cataloguing-in-Publication Data
A catalogue record for this book is available from the British Library.

ISBN: 978-1-78359-785-7

Printed in Great Britain by Ashford Colour Press Ltd, Gosport, Hampshire

Inter-Varsity Press publishes Christian books that are true to the Bible and that communicate
the gospel, develop discipleship and strengthen the church for its mission in the world.

IVP originated within the Inter-Varsity Fellowship, now the Universities and Colleges Christian
Fellowship, a student movement connecting Christian Unions in universities and colleges
throughout Great Britain, and a member movement of the International Fellowship of
Evangelical Students. Website: www.uccf.org.uk. That historic association is maintained,
and all senior IVP staff and committee members subscribe to the UCCF Basis of Faith.

Contents

Getting the Most Out of
The Twelve Disciples

It sounds like a crazed reality television show. You have to pick twelve people from hundreds of applicants. One of them will crash out of the program at a crucial moment—and betray the leader in the process. The remaining eleven will be responsible to carry a new spiritual movement to the ends of the earth. The people you will choose aren't necessarily the brightest and the best. They don't have advanced degrees from upscale universities. Most of them work with their hands in blue-collar jobs. At least one is a low-level government bureaucrat. The sharpest member of the group is quietly sabotaging the entire operation.

That scenario (from a purely human perspective) is what Jesus faced when he chose twelve men to be his closest followers. He had about three years to mold a dozen fearful and faithless men into the pillars of a worldwide movement. But Jesus had one advantage as he made his choice. He knew that the time they spent with him would have a transforming effect on each of these men. All of them would be changed by Jesus' power. Eleven would become outspoken witnesses of Jesus' redeeming grace—and even the betrayer would be changed by his exposure to Jesus. His spirit would harden and become calloused to the power of love.

This study of Jesus' followers will change you too! You will discover that the Master is still in the business of transforming lives. He can take the most fear-filled and faithless among us and empower us to be confident witnesses of his grace and forgiveness.

I would challenge you, however, to think carefully about this journey before you get started. Make sure you are ready and willing to answer Jesus' call to follow him. It will be a journey you will never forget.

Becoming Disciples

Jesus had many disciples. At the height of his popularity, large crowds followed him. But within the larger group of followers, Jesus had smaller groups of men and women who were more deeply committed to him. He had seventy-two disciples, for example, who were sent out in pairs to preach the good news of the kingdom (Lk 10:1, 17). A group of faithful women were with Jesus at times, and some of them helped support his ministry financially (Mk 15:40-41; Lk 8:1-3).

The most well-known of Jesus' disciples, of course, were the Twelve—twelve men chosen by Jesus after a night of prayer (Lk 6:12-13). They were called to travel with Jesus full-time and to be eyewitnesses of his ministry. They also were commissioned to preach and to cast out evil spirits as evidence that Jesus was Israel's promised Messiah. There are four lists of the Twelve in the New Testament (Mt 10:2-4; Mk 3:16-19; Lk 6:14-16; Acts 1:13). Some of the Twelve appear often in the Gospel accounts; a few are only mentioned once or twice. The goal of this study is to focus on each man and how each one was changed because of his association with Jesus.

Sent Out

The twelve disciples are also called *apostles* in the New Testament. An apostle was a person sent out by a king or governor with an important message. The "sent one" spoke with all the authority of the sender. When Jesus sent these men into the world with the good news of God's grace and forgiveness, they spoke with the authority of Jesus himself. It was the writings of the apostles and their close associates that laid the foundation of the church. We who follow Jesus today believe on the basis of the testimony of these witnesses.

So we can expect to grow as disciples as we study how Jesus made disciples, and we can expect to hear a new call in our lives to follow Christ with a whole heart. Then we can expect to be sent out into the world to make disciples of all nations—including our workplace and neighborhood. Exposure to Jesus always brings transformation!

Suggestions for Individual Study

1. As you begin each study, pray that God will speak to you through his Word.

2. Read the introduction to the study and respond to the personal reflection question or exercise. This is designed to help you focus on God and on the theme of the study.

3. Each study deals with a particular passage so that you can delve into the author's meaning in that context. Read and reread the passage to be studied. The questions are written using the language of the New International Version, so you may wish to use that version of the Bible. The New Revised Standard Version is also recommended.

4. This is an inductive Bible study, designed to help you discover for yourself what Scripture is saying. The study includes three types of questions. Observation questions ask about the basic facts: who, what, when, where and how. Interpretation questions delve into the meaning of the passage. Application questions help you discover the implications of the text for growing in Christ. These three keys unlock the treasures of Scripture.

Write your answers to the questions in the spaces provided or in a personal journal. Writing can bring clarity and deeper understanding of yourself and of God's Word.

5. It might be good to have a Bible dictionary handy. Use it to look up any unfamiliar words, names or places.

6. Use the prayer suggestion to guide you in thanking God for what you have learned and to pray about the applications that have come to mind.

7. You may want to go on to the suggestion under "Now or Later," or you may want to use that idea for your next study.

Suggestions for Members of a Group Study

1. Come to the study prepared. Follow the suggestions for individual study mentioned above. You will find that careful preparation will greatly enrich your time spent in group discussion.

2. Be willing to participate in the discussion. The leader of your group will not be lecturing. Instead, he or she will be encouraging the members of the group to discuss what they have learned. The leader will be asking the questions that are found in this guide.

3. Stick to the topic being discussed. Your answers should be based on the verses which are the focus of the discussion and not on outside authorities such as commentaries or speakers. These studies focus on a particular passage of Scripture. Only rarely should you refer to other portions of the Bible. This allows for everyone to participate in in-depth study on equal ground.

4. Be sensitive to the other members of the group. Listen attentively when they describe what they have learned. You may be surprised by their insights! Each question assumes a variety of answers. Many questions do not have "right" answers, particularly questions that aim at meaning or application. Instead the questions push us to explore the passage more thoroughly.

When possible, link what you say to the comments of others. Also, be affirming whenever you can. This will encourage some of the more hesitant members of the group to participate.

5. Be careful not to dominate the discussion. We are sometimes so eager to express our thoughts that we leave too little opportunity for others to respond. By all means participate! But allow others to also.

6. Expect God to teach you through the passage being discussed and through the other members of the group. Pray that you will have an enjoyable and profitable time together, but also that as a result of the study you will find ways that you can take action individually and/or as a group.

7. Remember that anything said in the group is considered confidential and should not be discussed outside the group unless specific permission is given to do so.

8. If you are the group leader, you will find additional suggestions at the back of the guide.

1

Andrew

Bringing Others to Jesus

John 1:35-42

I would like to have Andrew as a brother. If I had known Jesus' closest followers personally, I might have gone to Nathanael for a Bible study or to Matthew for investment advice, but for a friend, a brother who would love me no matter what, I would have chosen Andrew.

Andrew was not one of the major players among the twelve disciples. In fact, he always seems to play a supporting role. In most of his appearances, however, he is bringing someone else to Jesus.

I am starting this study of the Twelve with Andrew because Jesus starts with him. According to the New Testament, Andrew was the first of the Twelve to follow Jesus. In the early centuries of the church Andrew was called *protokletos* (proto-**clay**-toss), a Greek word that means "first-called"—and the first thing Andrew did after he believed was look for his brother.

GROUP DISCUSSION. What qualities would you look for in someone who is truly a "brother" or a "sister"? If you are comfortable doing it, share with the group who that person is in your life.

PERSONAL REFLECTION. Who are the people you think of as a "brother" or "sister"—people you have a close, trusting relationship with? What can you do this week to strengthen (or to cultivate) that relationship?

Andrew was on a search. He had a deep spiritual hunger and wanted the Lord to have the primary place in his heart and mind. Andrew was a disciple of John the Baptist and had absorbed this eccentric preacher's message of repentance and preparation. One day Andrew saw John point to a man at the edge of the crowd. "Look," John said, "the Lamb of God, who takes away the sin of the world!" (Jn 1:29). The next day Andrew and an unnamed disciple (probably John the son of Zebedee) left the Baptist and began to follow Jesus. *Read John 1:35-42.*

---

1. From what you read in this passage, give a brief description of each person's role in the story.

John the Baptist

Jesus

Andrew

the other disciple

Simon Peter

---

2. How do you think John felt when two of his followers left him and began following Jesus (v. 37)?

---

3. Explain what Jesus meant when he asked, "What do you want?" Was it a simple question or more than that?

---

4. What prompted you to seek after Jesus—curiosity, the faith of your parents, a Christian friend, the testimony of the Bible? Explain the factors that drew you to faith or interest in Jesus.

5. The first thing Andrew did when he was convinced that Jesus was the promised Messiah was to find his brother, Simon (vv. 41-42). As a child, what did it take to convince you that something your brother or sister (or closest friend) told you was true?

Why do you think Simon might have struggled with Andrew's announcement?

6. Why is it sometimes difficult to talk to our family members (or closest friends) about a commitment to Jesus?

7. What can we do if those closest to us reject Jesus' offer of forgiveness and salvation?

8. Later, when Jesus called Andrew away from his fishing career to full-time discipleship, Andrew dropped what he was doing and followed Jesus (Mt 4:19-20). What does that response to discipleship tell you about the sincerity of Andrew's commitment here in John 1?

Share a time when you sensed Jesus calling you to a new level of commitment to him. How did you respond to that discipleship call?

9. In every later reference to Andrew in the New Testament, he is called "Simon Peter's brother." Everyone knew Peter; not as many knew Andrew. What does that tell you about Andrew's character and attitude?

---

10. What qualities in Andrew do you admire most and why?

Which one of these do you want to begin to develop or develop further in your own character?

Ask the Lord to give you a willingness to continue to say yes to him.

Now or Later

Three countries claim Andrew as their patron saint: Russia, Scotland and Greece. Church tradition says that Andrew died at Patrae, Greece. The local governor was so enraged that his wife and brother had become Christians that he condemned Andrew to be crucified. Andrew is said to have asked to be executed on an X-shaped cross, feeling unworthy to die on the same shaped cross as Jesus. The X-shaped cross has been known ever since as Saint Andrew's cross. Andrew lingered on the cross for almost three days, and during hours of consciousness he urged those looking on to believe in Jesus.

Think of one or two family members or friends who have not received Jesus as Savior and Lord. Begin to pray regularly for an open door of opportunity to talk with them. Then, when God opens the door, courageously walk through it.

2

Simon Peter

Defending (and Rebuking) the Savior

Mark 1:16-20; 8:27-38

We know more about Simon Peter than about any of the other disciples—but even his names reveal some of the issues he struggled with. Simon was his personal name; it meant "impulsive," "unsteady." Jesus is the one who gave him the name Peter or "rock"; Jesus saw what the man would become.

GROUP DISCUSSION. What descriptive name do you think Jesus would give you and why?

PERSONAL REFLECTION. Do you evaluate yourself as a follower of Jesus in light of the past, the present or the future? What can you do to focus yourself more on the potential that Jesus sees in you rather than on past failures or present struggles?

The Gospels are full of stories about Peter. He is always on stage, either at the center of things or waiting to insert himself in almost every scene. He acts and speaks impulsively and often puts his foot squarely in his mouth. Occasionally, however, Peter gets it right.

Some of the most startling declarations about Jesus and loyalty to
Jesus come from the lips of Peter—and then in the next breath he
is denying or correcting Jesus or even, as we will see in this study,
rebuking Jesus.

Peter's call to be a committed follower of Jesus is recorded in all four
Gospels. He had been acquainted with Jesus for several months, but
now he responds to Jesus' call to leave his former life behind. *Read
Mark 1:16-20.*

---

1. What task does Jesus call Simon and Andrew to (v. 17), and what
are they willing to leave behind as they follow him?

---

2. Peter and the other three men had met Jesus before this and had
spent time with him (Jn 1:35-42; 2:1-11). Why do you think they were
now willing to embrace this new level of loyalty to Jesus?

---

3. *Read Mark 8:27-38.* This encounter took place at about the midpoint
of Jesus' three-year public ministry. The opinions of other people
about Jesus were really quite flattering. What about Jesus' ministry
would have led people to conclude that he was:

the revived John the Baptist?

Elijah?

one of God's prophets?

What was lacking in these opinions of Jesus?

4. The disciples had been with Jesus more than a year. Why was Jesus so interested in their conclusions about who he was?

How would you personally answer Jesus' question—who is he to you?

5. Why do you think Jesus tells the disciples to keep quiet about his identity?

6. What does Jesus talk about next, and why is he so intent to communicate this truth to these men?

7. Why does Peter rebuke Jesus? How was Jesus' teaching different from what Peter expected?

8. What temptation from Satan does Jesus perceive in Peter's rebuke (v. 33)?

9. Jesus' rebuke of Peter is followed by his dramatic teaching to his disciples and to the crowd about the cost and the gain of following him (vv. 34-38). What is Jesus trying to get Peter (and all his followers) to realize about discipleship?

---

10. What change do you think Jesus wanted to see in Peter as the result of this encounter?

What change does Jesus want to see in you because of your exposure to this passage?

Prayerfully read Jesus' call to discipleship in verses 34-38 and ask Jesus to give you a willing spirit to follow him fully.

Now or Later

The almost unanimous testimony of the early church is that Peter went to Rome around A.D. 61 and was martyred there, condemned to death by emperor Nero. Several legends eventually emerged about Peter's death, but our most reliable testimony comes from the early church historian Eusebius. He says that Peter's wife was crucified first and that Peter was forced to watch her death. Peter conducted himself with such courage that his Roman jailer was moved to believe in Jesus. When it came time for his execution, Peter asked to be crucified head down and feet up since he did not consider himself worthy to die as his Lord had. In the end Peter gave his life as a testimony of his faith in and loyalty to Jesus.

What would you want your family and friends to say about you after you die? What are you doing right now to build that testimony?

3

Matthew

Drawing in the Outcast

Matthew 9:9-13

Matthew was the most notorious sinner in Jesus' band! His occupation was collecting taxes for the hated Roman overlords. Tax collectors worked for Rome in oppressing and exploiting their own people. In Jesus' day, employees of the Roman IRS were viewed as traitors, cheaters and thieves. They were the lowest of the low.

GROUP DISCUSSION. In your opinion, what are some less-than-respectable jobs for Christians to pursue?

PERSONAL REFLECTION. Have you ever thought someone was so bad that they were beyond God's forgiveness? The apostle Paul called himself the "worst of sinners" (1 Tim 1:6). Reflect on your own lost condition before Christ saved you.

In Mark 2:14, Matthew is called by his Jewish name, "Levi son of Alphaeus." In Luke 6:15 and Acts 1:13 he is called Matthew. He is the author of the first Gospel in our New Testament, but he only mentions himself twice by name—in Matthew 9 and in the list of the apostles in Matthew 10:3. *Read Matthew 9:9-13.*

1. Which is most surprising to you about this encounter between Jesus and Matthew: that Jesus identifies with some unacceptable people, that Matthew throws a party, or that the religious leaders are upset? Explain.

2. Matthew undoubtedly had contact with Jesus before this day. He probably heard Jesus teach in Capernaum or had seen Jesus heal the sick. What does it tell you about Matthew's level of commitment to Jesus that he was prepared to leave his old life behind and follow Jesus when he called?

3. What criticism might Jesus have heard when he included a tax collector among his closest followers?

What would Matthew's inclusion among Jesus' disciples communicate to those who thought they were too sinful to change?

4. What does it communicate to our culture when notorious sinners are transformed by Jesus and rise to places of leadership?

What kind of accusations of our leaders should we be ready to address?

---

5. The first thing Matthew does as a follower of Jesus is throw a party. How would you describe Matthew's friends in today's setting?

---

6. Do you think Jesus was uncomfortable in that setting? Explain.

How would you feel and act as the guest of honor at this gathering?

---

7. Write down the six or seven key terms Jesus uses in his response to the Pharisees (vv. 12-13).

Why do you think he used these terms?

---

8. Was Jesus calling the Pharisees "healthy" and "righteous"? Explain.

9. Do you think Matthew regretted his decision to leave his old life behind? Why or why not?

---

10. What might Jesus be asking you to leave behind in order to follow him more fully?

Ask the Lord to help you see people around you not just as they are but as they can be when transformed by Christ's love.

Now or Later

Volunteer individually or as a group to minister to people in need in your community: soup kitchens, food pantries and clothing centers often welcome help. Go with one intention—to demonstrate Christ's love and concern. Watch for a "Matthew" among those you see.

The church father Jerome called Matthew a man "who changed from a tax-gatherer to an apostle." He also says that Matthew was the first apostle in Judea to write a Gospel of Jesus Christ in Hebrew. Matthew's heart was for his own people, the Jews, and tradition says he preached Jesus to the Jews in Judea, Persia and perhaps Ethiopia. No reliable record survives of Matthew's death, but the earliest traditions say that he was burned at the stake for his faith.

4

James

Hating Our Enemies

Luke 9:51-56; Acts 12:1-2

Nicknames can be fun or cruel. My younger brother and I called our older brother "Fungus"—but usually not to his face. Jesus gave two of his disciples a nickname. He called James and John "sons of thunder"—a reflection of their passionate, zealous, sometimes stormy personalities.

GROUP DISCUSSION. Have you ever had a nickname? Did it accurately reflect anything about you? Just for fun, come up with a nickname for your study group.

PERSONAL REFLECTION. Think back to the names you were called in your younger years. Were they expressions of love or hurtful arrows? What memories do those names recall?

Even though James was one of the three disciples in Jesus' inner circle, he is one of the least familiar of the Twelve. James never appears alone in the Gospels. He is always linked with his better-known brother, John.

We get a glimpse of why James was a "son of thunder" in this account of a journey Jesus and his men took through Samaria. Jesus sent some men ahead to find lodging in a Samaritan village. *Read Luke 9:51-56.*

1. Where was Jesus going and what significant events were on the horizon of his life?

2. The Jews and the Samaritans were cultural enemies in Jesus' day, but Jesus had never shown anything but good will toward Samaritans. Describe the Samaritans' response to Jesus and his men.

How do you handle it when someone rejects you because of personal prejudice or for some other petty reason?

3. What does the suggestion from James and John tell you about their normal approach to obstacles or obstinate people?

What kind of spiritual leaders would they have been at this point?

4. What do you think Jesus rebuked them for? Their zeal? Their attitude? Their own prejudices? Explain.

5. What was Jesus trying to cultivate in James by his rebuke and his response of moving on to another village?

---

6. What attitude or quick reaction in you might Jesus single out for rebuke? What would Jesus say to you?

---

7. In *The Message*, Eugene Peterson translates rebuke as "exposing our rebellion" (2 Tim 3:16). What is the value of exposing rebellion in the lives of those you may seek to disciple to be followers of Jesus?

What are some guidelines for the use of rebuke?

---

8. *Read Acts 12:1-2.* James was the first apostle to be killed for his faith. Herod Agrippa I arrested both James and Peter (Acts 12:3), but Peter was miraculously delivered from Herod's prison. How would you explain to other Christians why God spared Peter but not James?

---

9. In what ways do you want to be like James?

What aspects of James's early character do you want to avoid or correct in your life?

Commit any prejudice or short-tempered reactions to the Lord. Ask the Holy Spirit to help you have self-control over anger or judgment toward others.

Now or Later

Eusebius, an early church historian, passes on this account of James's death:

> [The man] who led James to the judgment-seat [for trial], when he saw him bearing his testimony, was moved and confessed that he himself was also a Christian. They were both therefore led away together; and on the way he begged James to forgive him. And [James] after considering a little, said, "Peace be with thee," and kissed him. And thus they were both beheaded at the same time.*

What response would the "old" James have made to this request for forgiveness?

---

*Eusebius Pamphilius, *Church History*, 2.9.2-3, Nicene and Post-Nicene Church Fathers, ser. 2, vol. 1, ed. Philip Schaff (Grand Rapids: Eerdmans, 1956), www.ccel.org/ccel/schaff/npnf201.iii.vii.x.html.

5

Philip

Learning to Trust

John 6:1-13

If we want to understand the disciple named Philip, we need to start with his name. Though Philip grew up in a Jewish home, he had a distinctly non-Jewish name. Philip is a Greek name and means "lover of horses." This disciple never rides a horse that we know of, but the Greek roots of his name are significant. Some scholars have suggested that he was named after the best of Herod the Great's sons, Herod Philip II, who ruled an area northeast of the Sea of Galilee. Perhaps our man Philip's father was involved in the governmental bureaucracy and wanted to honor the man who was a fair and righteous ruler. It could be that Philip grew up in a home that was more open to non-Jewish friends than the typical Jewish home.

His name may have been why some Greeks who wanted to meet Jesus came to him Philip (Jn 12:20-22). They must have thought that Philip would be more open to their request. Philip was not in Jesus' inner circle, but in every New Testament list of the Twelve Philip is listed fifth. He was not a leader in the company of the disciples, but he was an important player on the second string.

GROUP DISCUSSION. Do you feel more comfortable in a leadership role or in a supporting role? Tell the group a story that illustrates your preference.

PERSONAL REFLECTION. How do you feel when you work hard on a project and someone else gets the credit? How do you express those feelings?

In the Gospels of Matthew, Mark and Luke, Philip is only a name on the roster of the Twelve. But John's Gospel rescues Philip from obscurity. Philip was probably a fisherman by trade, like Peter and Andrew, but he would have functioned best in an accounting office. Philip had a calculator for a mind, and Jesus wanted to temper that analytical bent with a strong dose of trust in God. *Read John 6:1-13.*

1. How would you describe to a friend the setting of this account and each character or group involved?

What about the scene makes it seem like an impossible situation?

2. Why were the crowds following Jesus?

What are some of the reasons people follow Jesus today?

Why do you follow him?

3. Jesus specifically asked Philip, "Where shall we buy bread for these people to eat?" But John makes it clear that Jesus was testing Philip (v. 6). What was Jesus looking for from Philip?

_____

4. What does Philip's answer tell you about how he approached tough life situations?

_____

5. Philip tried to figure out exactly how this situation could be resolved, but he calculated without faith in Jesus' power or ability to provide. Describe a time when you have tried to help the Lord out and how it ended.

_____

6. Rewrite Philip's response in a way that includes an expression of confident trust in Jesus' ability to meet this need.

_____

7. What do you think was the significance to Philip that there was more food left after everyone had eaten (twelve baskets [v. 13]) than they had before they began (five small loaves and two dried fish [v. 9])?

What does that say to you about how to face difficult situations in your life?

8. Consider the qualities that increased in Philip's character and the flaws that decreased after this incident. Complete the following sentences:

• After this incident, Philip was *more* . . .

• . . . and he was *less* . . .

---

9. What situation in your life do you need to trust God to work out?

Be specific in your gratitude to God each day—and more confident in Jesus' power to meet every challenge.

Now or Later

Church tradition says that Philip was a powerful preacher in the early church. The apostle Philip should not be confused with the *deacon* Philip, who is prominent in the early chapters of Acts. Philip the deacon witnessed to the Ethiopian government official (Acts 8:26-40) and is the only person called an "evangelist" in the New Testament (Acts 21:8). Within ten years of Jesus' resurrection, the *apostle* Philip was preaching in the Roman province of Phrygia in Asia Minor. He was stoned to death or perhaps crucified for his faith at the city of Hierapolis.

Jesus was able to take a man who had a very practical bent and add the dimension of faith to his gifts to create one of the foundational personalities of the church. Think about your gifts and abilities and inclinations. How can you offer these gifts in a new way to Jesus? Where can your abilities be used to strengthen or expand the church? Take one step to put your abilities to use in Christ's work.

6

John

Seeking to Be the Greatest

The Bible paints a dramatic "before and after" picture of John the apostle. In his later years John was called the apostle of love. In his New Testament writings John uses the word *love* eighty times. He gave us the best-known verse in the Bible: "For God so loved the world" (Jn 3:16). And from John we learn Jesus' new command to "love one another" (Jn 13:34) and hear the great declaration that "God is love" (1 Jn 4:8).

But John was not always a man marked by love. He and his older brother, James, were called "sons of thunder" by Jesus, and they threatened to call down fire from heaven on those who insulted them. In his early years John was quick to judge and was set on revenge against anyone who didn't agree with him.

GROUP DISCUSSION. We as Christians are commanded to love one another. Why is that so difficult to do?

PERSONAL REFLECTION. Reflect on how you have changed over the years. What has brought about the change? Have you mellowed or become hard? In what areas do you still need to change?

John's early spirit of pride and self-promotion revealed itself one day when his mother asked Jesus for special privileges. Jesus' response may have been the factor that started John down the long path of transformation and change. *Read Matthew 20:20-28.*

---

1. What does the passage tell us about how each person or group reacted to John's mother's request? Imagine the look on each one's face.

John and James:

The other disciples:

Jesus:

---

2. Rewrite this mother's request in the context of today. What was she really asking for?

---

3. Do you think John's mother made this request on her own or was she put up to it? Explain.

---

4. What did Jesus mean when he asked John and James if they were prepared to "drink the cup" Jesus would drink (v. 22)?

Was their answer honest? Was it realistic?

---

5. How does Jesus characterize the leadership of people in authority in the world (v. 25)?

Share an incident from your own experience in which you saw a boss or political figure "lord it over" someone.

---

6. How do authority and influence reveal themselves in the realm of Christ's kingdom (vv. 26-27)?

---

7. Jesus points to himself as the model of this kind of servant leadership. What qualified Jesus "to be served" by others?

---

8. In what ways are you expecting others to serve you?

How did Jesus serve instead?

9. In what ways are you serving others?

Ask God to reveal the potential he sees in you in the realm of servant leadership. Be willing to pursue the transformation that Jesus points out to you.

Now or Later

Reliable church tradition says that John lived a long life in the city of Ephesus. He was the only apostle to die a natural death. As an old man he was exiled to the prison island of Patmos, where he received the visions recorded in the book of Revelation. John also was moved by the Holy Spirit to write the Gospel of John and the three New Testament letters of John. The church father Irenaeus says that John died a natural death during the reign of the emperor Trajan (ruled A.D. 98-117).

Another church father, Jerome, recorded several centuries later that in his last years John was carried to church by the young men of the community. John would simply say to the gathered Christians, "Little children, love one another, love one another, love one another."

Using Jesus as your example, what one act can you do today to serve another person in love?

7

Thomas

Leaving Doubt Behind

John 20:19-29

Thomas had a scientific mind. Those of us who live in the modern world are conditioned to think that way by our education and culture. Thomas was just wired that way. He was more skeptical than most people, more demanding of proof. Before he accepted the word of others, he wanted to see for himself. That's why he has been called "doubting Thomas" all these centuries. He could believe—but only after the facts were in.

GROUP DISCUSSION. Are you mostly trusting or mostly skeptical of what you hear or read? Give an example of how you normally respond to new information.

PERSONAL REFLECTION. Are you a trusting person or do you tend to mistrust other people? How has that tendency helped or hindered your walk with the Lord?

Thomas is mentioned only by name in the first three Gospels. We get all the biblical information we have about him from the Gospel of John. The best known story about Thomas happens just after Jesus' resurrection. *Read John 20:19-29.*

1. What about Jesus' appearance to the disciples demonstrates that something supernatural was going on?

What does Jesus do to demonstrate that he is not a hallucination or dream, and why is that significant?

---

2. Jesus bestowed several gifts on his disciples. Explain what each one would have meant to these men who had seen their world crushed but now saw Jesus alive.

peace (v. 21):

a commission (v. 21):

empowerment (v. 22):

authority to proclaim forgiveness (v. 23):

---

3. Why do you think Thomas responded like he did to the news of Jesus' appearance?

4. How long did Jesus wait before he appeared to Thomas? What insight does that give you about how to approach a skeptic or even a Christian who is struggling with doubt?

5. What does Jesus do to assuage Thomas's doubt?

How has God worked in your life in times of doubt or uncertainty?

6. What is significant about Thomas's response to Jesus (v. 28)?

7. What is significant about Jesus' willingness to receive Thomas's tribute?

8. On what evidence do you rely for your belief that Jesus rose from the dead?

9. Three times Jesus blesses his disciples with peace (vv. 19, 21, 26). Where could you use Jesus' peace in your life right now?

---

10. How do you think Thomas changed after this encounter with Jesus?

Ask God to give you the confidence Thomas had to declare that Jesus is "my Lord and my God."

Now or Later

What resources have you found helpful when you have doubts—the Bible, books that explore the issues, the encouragement of other Christians, prayer? Explain how you go about dealing with doubts that arise in your mind.

According to the most reliable traditions, Thomas took the message of Jesus as far east as India. When the Portuguese explorer, Vasco da Gama reached India around A.D. 1500, he found a fellowship of churches that identified themselves as the Christians of Saint Thomas. A major Christian group in India has carried Thomas's name for centuries, the Mar Thoma church. Thomas is the only one of the Twelve to have a denomination named for him.

Tradition also says that Thomas died a martyr's death near the city of Chennai in India, on a mountain that still bears the name, St. Thomas Mount. His death came by the piercing of a lance.

8

Nathanael

Developing Spiritual Insight

John 1:43-51

The well-loved author Madeleine L'Engle had what she called her "special place" near her New England home. A brisk ten-minute walk beyond her own garden, past a willow tree and through a pasture brought her to a small brook and a natural stone bridge. She would sit in the grass or dangle her feet in the water as the tensions of life gradually eased away.

Nathanael had a quiet spot too. Jesus said that he saw Nathanael "under the fig tree" (Jn 1:48). For many people in Galilee the fig tree, traditionally planted near the front door of a house, was a place of quiet for rest or study or prayer. Since most homes had only one or two rooms, the spreading branches of a fig tree were where a person retreated for privacy and solitude.

GROUP DISCUSSION. In what place do you feel closest to God? Why?

PERSONAL REFLECTION. Do you have a quiet place where you go regularly to pray or read? What can you do to create such a space or to make the one you have more conducive to quiet meditation?

The name Bartholomew is listed among the Twelve in every New Testament list. The fourth Gospel, however, doesn't mention Bartholomew but tells us about Nathanael. It seems that they are the same person. Bartholomew could be Nathanael's second name since it means "son of Tolmai." Nathanael ("gift of God") was probably his personal name or a name Jesus gave him. The Bible tells us very little about this man, but it gives us more details about Nathanael's first encounter with Jesus and his call to follow Jesus than that of any other disciple. *Read John 1:43-51.*

---

1. Skim through the passage again and write down all the names and titles used to describe Jesus.

Which of these titles is most meaningful to you right now and why?

---

2. What insight about Jesus was most exciting to Philip (v. 45), and why?

---

3. Why did Nathanael find it hard to believe Philip's statement?

---

4. What prejudices or stereotypes prevent people today from trusting Jesus?

5. What does Jesus' assessment of Nathanael tell you about the character of this man (v. 47)?

Imagine what Jesus would say about you if he made an honest assessment of your life and character. How would it make you feel?

---

6. Nathanael responds to Jesus' words with skepticism until Jesus reveals that he had seen Nathanael in the private place of prayer and study "under the fig tree." Why was that such a convincing remark to Nathanael?

---

7. What convinced you to be a follower of Jesus?

---

8. Once Nathanael commits himself to Jesus, what does Jesus promise him (vv. 50-51)?

9. Have you gained deeper insight into who Jesus is since you first made a commitment to him? How has that insight come to you?

How do you demonstrate that Jesus is the Lord and King of your life?

Seek to make a firm commitment to Jesus as Lord, as King and as Son of God.

Now or Later

Students of the Gospels have struggled to identify exactly who Nathanael was. An early church father Epiphanius says that Nathanael was one of the men on the road to Emmaus who had an encounter with the resurrected Jesus (Lk 24:13-35). In that scene two disciples meet up with Jesus. One of the men is called Cleopas; the other man is not named.

A few interpreters of John's Gospel have identified Nathanael with Stephen, the deacon in the book of Acts who was stoned for his defense of Jesus as Israel's Messiah. That suggestion is based on Jesus' promise to Nathanael that he would see the heavens opened and the angels of God ascending and descending on the Son of Man (Jn 1:51). When Stephen was being stoned, he saw the heavens opened and Jesus standing at the right hand of God (Acts 7:56).

Some scholars do not think Nathanael was one of the Twelve at all. They see Nathanael as an expert in the law of Moses and the prophets. The fourth-century church father Augustine thought that an educated man like Nathanael would be excluded from Jesus' inner circle because Jesus wanted to change the world through ordinary, unlearned men.

The late William Barclay (who believed that Nathanael and

Bartholomew were the same person) summarized this apostle's character: "a man who was a seeking student, a man who was earnest in prayer, a man who made the complete surrender, and a man who became a man of action and one of the most adventurous missionaries in the history of the Church."[*]

Which of the aspects of Nathanael's character do you want to strengthen in your life? What steps will you take to begin that process?

---

[*]William Barclay, *The Master's Men* (Nashville: Abingdon Press, 1959), p. 116.

9

Judas Iscariot

Turning Away

*Matthew 26:14-30,
47-50; 27:1-10*

The most notorious of all the disciples—and the one universally scorned—is Judas Iscariot, the betrayer of Jesus. His name appears in every list of the apostles (except in Acts 1), and it always appears last. Eleven apostles are an encouragement to us because they show how common people can be used by God, even with all their failures, to do remarkable things. Judas, on the other hand, stands as a warning about the power of spiritual carelessness and pride, which can drag us away from loyalty to Christ.

Judas was as close to Jesus as humanly possible for three years. He heard every teaching; he saw every miracle. But in all that time his heart only grew harder. The other disciples were being transformed by Jesus into passionate followers; Judas was being changed too— into Satan's instrument of deceit and betrayal.

GROUP DISCUSSION. Have you ever had a friend or colleague that appeared to be loyal, but in the end was a betrayer? Share your story with the group. What emotions still come to the surface when you remember that person?

PERSONAL REFLECTION. Think back to any acts of betrayal or mistrust

you have committed. What have you done about confessing those
deeds to God and to those you hurt? What more can you do?

Judas's name is derived from the Hebrew name Judah. His surname,
Iscariot, means "man of Kerioth" and probably points to the town
of Kerioth Hezron in Judea as Judas's home town. If that identifi-
cation is correct, Judas was the only one of the apostles who did not
come from Galilee in the north. Judas must have been trusted and
well-liked in the group since he carried the money that paid for the
disciples' food and expenses. The only thing we know about Judas's
family is that his father's name was Simon (Jn 6:71).

Judas's call to follow Jesus is not recorded anywhere in Scripture,
but he followed Jesus willingly. Like most Jews of the day, Judas was
looking for the Messiah, and he believed Jesus was the promised One.
Judas had given his life to follow Jesus, but he never gave Jesus his
heart. Instead he sought out Jesus' enemies with one intention—to
betray Jesus for a bargain price. *Read Matthew 26:14-30.*

---

1. What evidence do you see in this passage that shows Judas's
treachery and hypocrisy toward Jesus?

What evidence do you see of Jesus' grace toward Judas?

---

2. Why do you think Jesus selected Judas in the first place to be one
of his closest followers?

3. *Read Matthew 26:47-50.* What sign did Judas use to single out Jesus, and how is that act a continuing demonstration of Judas's deceit and betrayal?

---

4. Put yourself in the garden as one of Jesus' followers. How would you have felt as the crowd approached and what do you think your reaction would have been?

---

5. *Read Matthew 27:1-10.* What evidence of Judas's sorrow for his actions do you find in this passage?

Do you think his repentance was genuine? Explain.

---

6. If Judas had come to you with the admission of verse 4, what would you have encouraged Judas to do?

---

7. What can you say to a friend who is feeling guilty and depressed over something he or she has done?

8. Over what issues or mistakes do people decide to kill themselves?

Is that ever a good choice? Why or why not?

---

9. How can we avoid being like Judas? (And if you say, "I could never do what he did," you may already be moving in that direction.)

Ask Jesus to keep your heart open and responsive to him. Thank him again for his grace to you.

Now or Later

Theologians have debated for two thousand years about Judas. Some Christians believe that Judas was never truly a believer, that he was a hypocrite from the beginning and that his false profession was finally revealed in his betrayal. They conclude that Judas was never saved. Other Christians believe that Judas was a genuine believer at the beginning but he gradually drifted away from faith, and in the end he made a deliberate act of apostasy from the Lord. He denied Christ and in the process renounced his faith. So, in their minds, Judas was a genuine believer who rejected God's grace and ultimately was lost.

Which of these views seems most consistent with the biblical evidence to you? Who can you talk with who might be able to give you more insight? What issues or difficulties are raised by the position you take?

10

Three Others

Faithful to the End

Luke 18:18-30

The Gospel writers give us the names of three other apostles, but not much more. If these men ever asked Jesus a question or had an extended conversation with him, Scripture does not record it.

But we do know that they were chosen by Jesus to be in the band of his closest followers, and like the others, these three had left their old lives behind to follow him. They served, went out and preached, and witnessed Jesus' miracles like the others. They were faithful to Jesus but were not major players in the Gospel record.

GROUP DISCUSSION. Do you know a Christian who serves the Lord sacrificially and faithfully, but quietly and out of the spotlight? Talk about that person to the group. What would you expect his or her reward from the Lord to be?

PERSONAL REFLECTION. Jesus placed a high value on the spiritual disciplines that we carry out in secret—like prayer or giving to the poor. Evaluate your own life and ask yourself whether you do things to be noticed by others or noticed by God alone.

James, the son of Alphaeus, is the ninth name in Luke's list of the Twelve (Lk 6:14-16). He is the second man among the apostles named James; the other is James, the brother of John and the son of Zebedee. In Mark 15:40 he is called "James the less" or "James the younger," an indication that this James was younger than James the son of Zebedee. In Mark 2:14, Levi or Matthew is also called the son of Alphaeus. It could be that James the younger was the brother of Matthew. If so, this would make a third set of brothers among the Twelve—Peter and Andrew, James the older and John, and now Matthew and James the younger.

Along with two men named James, there were also two men named Simon among Jesus' closest disciples—Simon Peter, of course, and a man called "Simon the Zealot" in Luke 6:15. Simon at one time had been a member of the political movement known as the Zealots, one of the best-known and most-feared political groups of Jesus' day. The Zealots hated the Romans, and their single objective was to push the Roman overlords out of Israel. That was Simon's background. Coming into contact with Jesus changed him. Simon's zeal became focused on a different kind of kingdom, a kingdom of justice and righteousness.

There were two men named Judas in Jesus' band too—Judas Iscariot and Judas son of James (Lk 6:16). This man is also called Thaddaeus (Mt 10:3). Judas Thaddaeus asks only one question of Jesus (at least that's all that is recorded about him). In John 14:22 he asks: "Lord, why do you intend to show yourself [reveal your true nature] to us and not to the world?" It wasn't a rebuke or a challenge, just a question.

Even though we don't have much written in the Gospels about these men, they are included in some of the scenes that involve all the disciples—like the day Jesus told a rich man to sell all his possessions and give the money to the poor! *Read Luke 18:18-30.*

---

1. What would have been the response of most people to a rich man who wanted to be involved with their ministry?

2. What does the ruler's question (v. 18) tell you about his view of eternal life?

What is Jesus' view on the subject (v. 27)?

3. The man claims to have obeyed God's commands since his boyhood. What was Jesus trying to get him to realize by asking him to sell his possessions (vv. 20-22)?

4. How do you think you would respond if Jesus made the same request of you?

5. Why is it hard for a rich person to enter the kingdom of God (vv. 24-25)?

6. Peter speaks for all of Jesus' disciples when he says, "We have left all we had to follow you!" Do you think Peter's statement was true? What specifically had the disciples left?

7. What promises does Jesus make to those who leave anything behind (or who put other relationships in second place) to do God's will (vv. 29-30)?

How have you experienced those promises in your life?

8. What one sacrifice is Jesus asking you to make?

9. Does it help to know that you will receive eternal rewards for the sacrifices you make for the Lord in this life? Explain.

As you pray, ask God to help you hold life's possessions in an open hand, ready to release them to the Lord when he asks.

Now or Later

Later church tradition reveals that these three virtually silent disciples took seriously Jesus' command to make disciples in every part of the world. We also learn that they paid the supreme price! James the younger took the message of Jesus to Syria and Persia. One tradition says that he was pushed from the temple wall in Jerusalem as he preached about Jesus, and the crowd below stoned him to death.

Several sources say that Simon the Zealot took the gospel as far north as Britain. Traditional portraits of Simon show him holding a saw because there are some legends that he was executed by being pushed into a hollow log and sawn in half.

Judas Thaddaeus is believed to have taken the gospel to eastern Turkey, to Persia, perhaps to China. The traditional symbol of this disciple is a club, because some sources say he was clubbed to death by an angry mob. Saint Jude (as he is usually referred to in the Roman Catholic Church) is the patron saint of desperate situations and the namesake of St. Jude's Children's Hospital in Memphis, Tennessee.

Which of the twelve followers of Jesus that we have studied do you think you are most like and why? Which one inspires you to follow Jesus more devotedly and why?

Leader's Notes

MY GRACE IS SUFFICIENT FOR YOU. (2 COR 12:9)

Leading a Bible discussion can be an enjoyable and rewarding experience. But it can also be *scary*—especially if you've never done it before. If this is your feeling, you're in good company. When God asked Moses to lead the Israelites out of Egypt, he replied, "O Lord, please send someone else to do it!" (Ex 4:13). It was the same with Solomon, Jeremiah and Timothy, but God helped these people in spite of their weaknesses, and he will help you as well.

You don't need to be an expert on the Bible or a trained teacher to lead a Bible discussion. The idea behind these inductive studies is that the leader guides group members to discover for themselves what the Bible has to say. This method of learning will allow group members to remember much more of what is said than a lecture would.

These studies are designed to be led easily. As a matter of fact, the flow of questions through the passage from observation to interpretation to application is so natural that you may feel that the studies lead themselves. This study guide is also flexible. You can use it with a variety of groups—student, professional, neighborhood or church groups. Each study takes forty-five to sixty minutes in a group setting.

There are some important facts to know about group dynamics and encouraging discussion. The suggestions listed below should enable you to effectively and enjoyably fulfill your role as leader.

Preparing for the Study

1. Ask God to help you understand and apply the passage in your own life. Unless this happens, you will not be prepared to lead others. Pray too for the various members of the group. Ask God to open your hearts to the message of his Word and motivate you to action.

2. Read the introduction to the entire guide to get an overview of the entire book and the issues which will be explored.

3. As you begin each study, read and reread the assigned Bible passage to familiarize yourself with it.

4. This study guide is based on the New International Version of the Bible. It will help you and the group if you use this translation as the basis for your study and discussion.

5. Carefully work through each question in the study. Spend time in meditation and reflection as you consider how to respond.

6. Write your thoughts and responses in the space provided in the study guide. This will help you to express your understanding of the passage clearly.

7. It might help to have a Bible dictionary handy. Use it to look up any unfamiliar words, names or places. (For additional help on how to study a passage, see chapter five of *How to Lead a LifeBuilder Study*, IVP, 2018.)

8. Consider how you can apply the Scripture to your life. Remember that the group will follow your lead in responding to the studies. They will not go any deeper than you do.

9. Once you have finished your own study of the passage, familiarize yourself with the leader's notes for the study you are leading. These are designed to help you in several ways. First, they tell you the purpose the study guide author had in mind when writing the study. Take time to think through how the study questions work together to accomplish that purpose. Second, the notes provide you with additional background information or suggestions on group dynamics for various questions. This information can be useful when people have difficulty understanding or answering a question. Third, the leader's notes can alert you to potential problems you may encounter during the study.

10. If you wish to remind yourself of anything mentioned in the leader's notes, make a note to yourself below that question in the study.

Leading the Study

1. Begin the study on time. Open with prayer, asking God to help the group to understand and apply the passage.

2. Be sure that everyone in your group has a study guide. Encourage the group to prepare beforehand for each discussion by reading the introduction to the guide and by working through the questions in the study.

3. At the beginning of your first time together, explain that these studies are meant to be discussions, not lectures. Encourage the members of the group to participate. However, do not put pressure on those who may be hesitant to speak during the first few sessions. You may want to suggest the following guidelines to your group.

☐ Stick to the topic being discussed.

☐ Your responses should be based on the verses which are the focus of the discussion and not on outside authorities such as commentaries or speakers.

☐ These studies focus on a particular passage of Scripture. Only rarely should you refer to other portions of the Bible. This allows for everyone to participate in in-depth study on equal ground.

☐ Anything said in the group is considered confidential and will not be discussed outside the group unless specific permission is given to do so.

☐ We will listen attentively to each other and provide time for each person present to talk.

☐ We will pray for each other.

4. Have a group member read the introduction at the beginning of the discussion.

5. Every session begins with a group discussion question. The question or activity is meant to be used before the passage is read. The question introduces the theme of the study and encourages group members to begin to open up. Encourage as many members as possible to participate, and be ready to get the discussion going with your own response.

This section is designed to reveal where our thoughts or feelings need to be transformed by Scripture. That is why it is especially important not to read the passage before the discussion question is asked. The passage will tend to color the honest reactions people would otherwise give because they are, of course, supposed to think the way the Bible does.

You may want to supplement the group discussion question with an icebreaker to help people to get comfortable. See the community section of the *Small Group Starter Kit* (IVP, 1995) for more ideas.

You also might want to use the personal reflection question with your group. Either allow a time of silence for people to respond individually or discuss it together.

6. Have a group member (or members if the passage is long) read aloud the passage to be studied. Then give people several minutes to read the passage again silently so that they can take it all in.

7. Question 1 will generally be an overview question designed to briefly survey the passage. Encourage the group to look at the whole passage, but try to avoid getting sidetracked by questions or issues that will be addressed later in the study.

8. As you ask the questions, keep in mind that they are designed to be used just as they are written. You may simply read them aloud. Or you may prefer to express them in your own words.

There may be times when it is appropriate to deviate from the study guide. For example, a question may have already been answered. If so, move on to the next question. Or someone may raise an important question not covered in the guide. Take time to discuss it, but try to keep the group from going off on tangents.

9. Avoid answering your own questions. If necessary, repeat or re-phrase them until they are clearly understood. Or point out something you read in the leader's notes to clarify the context or meaning. An eager group quickly becomes passive and silent if they think the leader will do most of the talking.

10. Don't be afraid of silence. People may need time to think about the question before formulating their answers.

11. Don't be content with just one answer. Ask, "What do the rest of you think?" or "Anything else?" until several people have given answers to the question.

12. Acknowledge all contributions. Try to be affirming whenever possible. Never reject an answer. If it is clearly off-base, ask, "Which verse led you to that conclusion?" or again, "What do the rest of you think?"

13. Don't expect every answer to be addressed to you, even though this will probably happen at first. As group members become more at ease, they will begin to truly interact with each other. This is one sign of healthy discussion.

14. Don't be afraid of controversy. It can be very stimulating. If you don't resolve an issue completely, don't be frustrated. Move on and keep it in mind for later. A subsequent study may solve the problem.

15. Periodically summarize what the group has said about the passage. This helps to draw together the various ideas mentioned and gives continuity to the study. But don't preach.

16. At the end of the Bible discussion you may want to allow group members a time of quiet to work on an idea under "Now or Later." Then discuss what you experienced. Or you may want to encourage group members to work on these ideas between meetings. Give an opportunity during the session for people to talk about what they are learning.

17. Conclude your time together with conversational prayer, adapting the prayer suggestion at the end of the study to your group. Ask for God's help in following through on the commitments you've made.

18. End on time.

Many more suggestions and helps are found in *How to Lead a LifeBuilder Study*.

Components of Small Groups

A healthy small group should do more than study the Bible. There are four components to consider as you structure your time together.

Nurture. Small groups help us to grow in our knowledge and love of God. Bible study is the key to making this happen and is the foundation of your small group.

Community. Small groups are a great place to develop deep friendships with other Christians. Allow time for informal interaction before and after each study. Plan activities and games that will help you get to know each other. Spend time having fun together going on a picnic or cooking dinner together.

Worship and prayer. Your study will be enhanced by spending time praising God together in prayer or song. Pray for each other's needs and keep track of how God is answering prayer in your group. Ask God to help you to apply what you are learning in your study.

Outreach. Reaching out to others can be a practical way of applying what you are learning, and it will keep your group from becoming self-focused. Host a series of evangelistic discussions for your friends or neighbors. Clean up the yard of an elderly friend. Serve at a soup kitchen together, or spend a day working in the community.

Many more suggestions and helps in each of these areas are found in the *Small Group Starter Kit*. You will also find information on building a small group. Reading through the starter kit will be worth your time.

Study 1. Andrew. John 1:35-42.

Purpose: To discover what it means to interest others in Jesus as it is modeled in Andrew's life.

Question 1. Every reference to "John" by name in this passage is a reference to John the Baptist. John the apostle, the son of Zebedee and the brother of James, is the author of this Gospel, but he never mentions himself by name.

Question 2. John the Baptist was the forerunner of the Messiah, the coming One. God had told him that he would recognize the Messiah by a sign—when John baptized him, the Spirit would descend and remain on him (Jn 1:29-34). Once John recognized that Jesus was the promised One, John began to point others to Jesus. So Andrew and the other disciple were not abandoning John to follow Jesus, but were acting on the fulfillment of what John had been teaching. John certainly understood this and encouraged their decision. Not all of John's followers left him; some stayed with him until his death (Mk 6:29).

Question 3. The author of this Gospel often writes on two levels. In one sense Jesus' question is just straight narrative. John is telling the story. But Jesus also wanted these men (and us) to reflect on a deeper level. It's as if Jesus confronts those who show any interest in following him and requires that they express what it is they really want in life. A possible follow-up question to your group might be: How would *you* answer Jesus' question?

The two disciples respond by calling Jesus "rabbi"—a title of honor and respect, a word that places these two men in the position of learners from Jesus. Jesus responds to them by inviting them to the place where he was staying for a more private and intense discussion. On one level Jesus was simply being friendly (a great first step in evangelism and disciple making); on another level Jesus was drawing these men into a deeper relationship with and commitment to him.

Question 4. This is a question that can reveal a lot about a person's relationship with Jesus. Let group members volunteer to answer. If no one does, ask the question a different way: Which of you were drawn to Jesus by childhood instruction or your parents' faith? Break the question into smaller pieces.

Question 5. Nothing directly points to any hesitation on Peter's part, but such an announcement would inevitably prompt questions: The *Messiah*? How do you know? Who is he? Andrew's actions and enthusiasm demonstrate that the most common and effective testimony to others is a private witness of a friend to a friend.

The term *messiah* is a transliteration of the Hebrew word meaning "anointed one." It was used in the Old Testament to describe anyone uniquely chosen by God for a special task. Andrew uses the word to refer to the "anointed one" in the fullest sense—the promised Deliverer sent from God. John translates the word for his readers into the Greek word *Christos* (from *chrio*, "to anoint). *Christ* is a title, not a name, given to Jesus.

Questions 6-7. Our family members and close friends know us best. They have seen our struggles and failures, and it's easy to feel like we are being pushy or preachy. If those closest to us reject Jesus, we can continue to pray for them and strive to model a genuine, Christ-centered life before them (see 1 Pet 3:1-2).

Question 8. Andrew's friendship with Jesus began at this point, but it also deepened over the months ahead. Andrew started down the path of discipleship and never looked back. At each new level of commitment, Andrew was ready to say yes to Jesus.

Question 9. Andrew was willing to live in his brother's shadow if it meant fulfilling God's purpose for him. He is like the children's worker or parent who leads a child to faith and then sees that child grow to become a fully committed disciple and perhaps God's instrument to reach many others with the gospel. Both individuals will share in Christ's reward for their faithfulness.

Study 2. Simon Peter. Mark 1:16-20; 8:27-38.
Purpose: To examine and begin to correct the inconsistencies between our Christian profession and our Christian life.

Introduction. The apostle Peter has four names in the New Testament. When he first appears on the scene, he is called Simon (Mk 1:16; Jn 1:40-41). This was his personal name, the name that came most quickly to the lips of the people who knew Peter best. (2) Twice in the New Testament Peter is called Simeon—by James in Acts 15:14 and at the beginning of Peter's second letter (2 Pet 1:1). Simeon is the original Hebrew form of the name Simon. (3) Jesus gave Simon the name Peter (Mk 3:16; Lk 6:14; Jn 1:42). The name Simon means "wavering"; the name Peter means "rock." Jesus would have a transforming impact on Peter. (4) Peter is called Cephas (**see**-fass) on several occasions. Cephas is the Aramaic word for rock and so became Peter's name when his friends conversed in Aramaic. The apostle Paul regularly uses the name Cephas to refer to Peter (1 Cor 1:12; 3:22; 15:5; Gal 2:9). In John's Gospel, Peter is referred to most often as Simon Peter (e.g., Jn 1:40; 6:68; 13:6, 24, 36).

Question 1. Fishing was a thriving industry around the Sea of Galilee in the first century. Peter and Andrew worked together as a team of fishermen. Now Jesus calls them to *become* fishers of men (literal translation of Mk 1:17). What they needed to learn and do would only be acquired as they followed Jesus. The process of becoming a disciple is slow and at times painful. Discipleship is always costly too. The nets of their business and the ties of their family must now be placed under their primary allegiance to Jesus. The goal of following Jesus was to draw others into a relationship with him. The rewards of this new vocation were eternal.

Question 2. It's clear from John 1:35-42 that Peter and Andrew and likely John had prior acquaintance with Jesus. These men were probably with Jesus at the wedding in Cana too (Jn 2:2). So Jesus did not walk up to men he had never met and call them to follow him out of the blue. Perhaps Jesus had told them that a call to a deeper commitment would be coming. Their motives for following him may have been to satisfy their own spiritual hunger or to have a place of prominence in the coming kingdom—or some combination of several motives.

Question 3. It was no small thing to be compared to some of the great men of Israel's past. The comparison to Elijah may have been made because Jesus, like Elijah, performed miracles or because the prophet Malachi had hinted that Elijah would return just before the day of the Lord would burst on the world scene (Mal 4:5-6). The comparison to one of the prophets may have come from Jesus' teaching ministry and his bold declaration of God's truth. Linking Jesus with John the Baptist may have emerged from Jesus' courageous confrontation with religious leaders about the lack of justice or mercy in Israel's culture. John the Baptist had already been executed by Herod Antipas (Mk 6:14-29), so Jesus would have to be a revived John or a prophet who took on the mantle of John's ministry after his death. The comparisons were all very flattering, but they fell short of grasping and explaining Jesus' true character and mission.

Question 4. Jesus had spent more than a year demonstrating to these men that he was the promised Messiah of Israel, God with us. Until they understood who Jesus is, they would not begin to comprehend what he had come to earth to do.

Allow participants in the group to voice their opinions about Jesus without judgment or correction. The goal, especially if you have unbelieving group members, is to find out exactly what they think about Jesus and then to compare what they think with who Jesus really is.

Question 5. Jesus' command to silence was a way of safeguarding his identity from being misused by those who would make him a king and stir up rebellion against Rome. Jesus' messiahship would be very different from the popular stereotype. Jesus was also concerned that the divine plan of redemption would unfold at the right time, not ahead of time. Jesus now begins to teach the true meaning of his mission—a view that Peter and the other disciples were unprepared to hear.

Question 6. The disciples had grasped that Jesus was the Messiah, but now they needed to have their understanding of what the Messiah would do corrected. Jesus would wrap himself in a servant's towel rather than a warrior's armor. He had not come to be served by others but to serve. He would not inflict suffering, but suffer himself as "a ransom for many" (Mk 10:45).

Question 7. Jesus' explanation of his own approaching suffering cut to the heart of what Peter expected from Israel's promised Deliverer. Peter saw Jesus' arrest and death as marks of failure and defeat, not the way to success and victory. No one in first-century Israel was saying that the Messiah should suffer. Jesus' words were scandalous! Jesus may have been willing to endure Peter's rebuke personally, but when he saw the other disciples listening, he rebuked Peter in return.

Question 8. Jesus uses the same words to rebuke Peter in verse 33 that he used against Satan himself in Matthew 4:10 when Jesus was tempted in the wilderness. Satan offered Jesus authority over all the kingdoms of the world. Jesus could avoid the pain and suffering of the cross and still be king. All Jesus had to do was worship Satan. In Peter's words Jesus heard the same subtle temptation to avoid the cross, and he refused to give in.

Question 9. A wrong view of messiahship leads to a wrong view of discipleship. If we follow Jesus as a path to recognition or wealth or prestige, we have the wrong view of what discipleship involves. Following Jesus means picking up a cross.

It's important to emphasize that Jesus is not talking in these verses about *salvation*; he's talking about becoming a *disciple*. We are saved by God's grace through faith; we follow Jesus in this world by losing our lives for him and for the gospel.

Study 3. Matthew. Matthew 9:9-13.

Purpose: To see Jesus' concern for those on the edges of society and to make his concern part of our vision for reaching others.

Introduction. "There was no class of men in the ancient world more hated than taxgatherers" (William Barclay, *The Master's Men* [Nashville: Abingdon Press, 1959], p. 59). In Israel a tax collector was barred from being a witness or a judge in a trial. He was also refused entrance to the courtyards near the temple for worship (which is why in Jesus' parable the tax collector stood "at a distance" to pray [Lk 18:13]). Because the Roman tax system allowed for excessive and unjust taxation, tax collectors were notorious for their greed. Because Matthew had his tax office in Capernaum, he technically worked for the Roman puppet-king over that area, Herod Antipas, rather than directly for Rome, but that made little difference in how he was regarded.

Question 2. It is highly unlikely that Jesus simply walked up out of the blue to Matthew and called him to follow. Most likely, Matthew had heard Jesus teach or had talked to some of Jesus' followers in Capernaum, like Peter or Andrew. However he heard, Matthew was convinced that Jesus was the Messiah, and he had already decided that when (and if) Jesus called him to follow him, he would go.

Question 3. Including a tax collector might have brought criticism against Jesus from two directions: the religious people would certainly see this as a sign that Jesus was not a godly man, and even the general public would find it difficult to accept the inclusion of this hated tax collector. On the other hand, if Jesus can call, change and use a tax collector, of all people, it gives the rest of us some hope too.

Question 4. Try not to let the discussion stray into specific sins or specific people, but keep it on the "what if" level. If the world sees a person who has failed be restored, loved and forgiven rather than kicked aside, it may give them hope of redemption as well.

Question 5. Let the group imagine Matthew's banquet in today's terms. Who were his friends? What might they bring to the party or do at the banquet that would make us feel uncomfortable?

Question 6. Jesus would have been perfectly at ease in this setting, without participating in anything sinful. These were the people Jesus came to reach! On the other hand, not every younger (or weaker) Christian can place themselves in a situation where he or she is tempted to sin. Every Christian needs to develop discernment and also needs to rely on the Spirit's direction. But we also should be sensitive to the people around us every day. We can demonstrate Christ's transforming power without putting ourselves in potentially compromising situations.

Question 7. Jesus answers the Pharisees with a series of wise sayings that reveal the true nature of his mission. It is not healthy people who need a doctor's care, but those who are sick. The Pharisees may have taken this as a compliment until they thought about it more deeply. Jesus as a spiritual doctor had come to care for those who were willing to admit that they needed his help. Then Jesus quoted Hosea 6:6 and admonished these experts in the Scriptures to learn what that verse really meant. God does not simply want the outward motions of worship (sacrifice); God examines the heart for evidence of the Spirit's transformation (mercy). Finally, Jesus makes it personal: "I have not come to call the righteous, but sinners." Jesus came to call everyone to salvation and discipleship, but he will focus his efforts on the people who are open to his call, not on those who believe they have no need of him.

Question 8. Jesus confronts these Pharisees very subtly through the use of irony. If you think you are spiritually healthy (as these men thought), you don't need Jesus. If you think you are right before God, Jesus will focus his attention on others who know they are sinners. This doesn't mean that Jesus was not interested in the salvation of the Pharisees. It simply meant that Jesus would wait until they came to the place of seeing their need of his mercy and grace.

Question 9. In order to join Jesus and the other disciples, Matthew left the security of a well-paying job and the company of friends who accepted him. He also left his old damaged reputation behind and started new as a follower of Jesus. There may have been brief moments when Matthew regretted his decision—when Jesus was arrested and crucified, for example—but overall Matthew seemed to become a zealous proclaimer of the message of Jesus' love. His passion was to reach his own people, the Jews, the very people who had regarded him with such hatred as a tax collector. Matthew's Gospel was written to grab the attention of a Jewish reader. Matthew quotes the Old Testament Scriptures more than the other three Gospel writers combined. The opening paragraph of his Gospel connects Jesus with the two great names in Israel's past—Abraham and David. Matthew presents Jesus as Israel's true King, the Messiah, the Son of the living God.

Study 4. James. Luke 9:51-56; Acts 12:1-2.

Purpose: To learn to be zealous for the Lord without walking over other people or calling down fire from heaven.

Introduction. James was probably the older of the two sons of Zebedee since his name is always given first when referring to both brothers. Several times in the Gospel accounts, James and John are simply called "the sons of Zebedee," which implies that Zebedee, their father, was a man of some importance and renown within the early Christian community. Zebedee had a fishing enterprise large enough to employ his two sons as well as hired workers (Mk 1:20). Mark is the Gospel writer who tells us that Jesus referred to the two brothers as *Boanerges* (bo-**an**-er-jeez), or "sons of thunder" (Mk 3:17).

In two of the New Testament lists of the apostles, James's name comes immediately after Peter's name. This placement implies that James was a strong leader in the Christian fellowship. He was also one of the three disciples who made up the inner circles of Jesus' apostles—Peter, James and his brother John.

Be sure you distinguish between the subject of our study—James the apostle, the brother of John, the son of Zebedee—and the author of the New Testament book of James. The book of James was most likely written by the half-brother of Jesus (Mk 6:3), who was also a leader in the Jerusalem church (Acts 15:13; Gal 1:19; Jas 1:1). Furthermore, another of Jesus' disciples was named James ("James the son of Alphaeus" [Lk 6:15]). Because so little is known about this third man named James, he is sometimes called "James the younger" or "less" (Mk 15:40), while James, the son of Zebedee, is called "James the Greater" or "James the Elder."

Question 1. This event takes place at the beginning of Jesus' journey to Jerusalem. He has resolutely set his heart and mind toward that city and the final events of his ministry that will unfold there. The opposition against Jesus has been rising for more than a year and is about to reach the crucial point. Jesus knows exactly what lies ahead. This rejection by the Samaritans is just a foreshadowing of the conflict Jesus will face in the coming days.

Question 2. The Jews of Jesus' day looked at Samaritans with contempt. In their minds the Samaritans were a mixed-race people who held to a corrupted view of God's law and were unworthy of heaven. The Samaritans in turn despised the Jews for their arrogance and condemnation. Jesus, however, had shown nothing but love and acceptance toward Samaritans:

- He healed a Samaritan's leprosy and commended the man for his thankful spirit (Lk 17:16).

- He made a Samaritan the hero of one of his best-known parables (Lk 10:30-37).

- He ministered to a Samaritan woman and offered her the water of life (Jn 4:7-29).

Jesus had always been kind to the Samaritans, yet this village of Samaritans was treating him with deliberate insult.

Question 3. The threat to call down fire from heaven had a biblical backdrop. In this same region of Old Testament Israel, the prophet Elijah called down fire to destroy his enemies (see 2 Kings 1). James and John must have thought they were on pretty solid biblical ground with their suggestion. They thought Jesus would be pleased, but it was the wrong thing to do. Jesus' mission was very different from Elijah's. Jesus came to save, not destroy.

Try not to let the discussion about spiritual leaders stray into names of heavy-handed leaders or even personal experiences that don't shed light on the character of James.

Question 4. Jesus' rebuke to James and John probably centered on their own motives in suggesting fire from heaven. There was more than a touch of arrogance in what they said—"Lord, do you want *us* to call fire down?" James and John didn't have that power, only Jesus did. If it had been the right thing to do, Jesus would have done it. He undoubtedly also rebuked them for their lack of compassion for the people of the village. The people were insulting, but they were also people Jesus came to reach with his grace.

Question 5. Jesus wanted James to see that the best approach to personal insult is to absorb the pain and move to a more open situation. Arguing with or condemning people rarely leads them to Christ. If they refuse the message, move on to those who are more open to hearing it.

Question 6. Be careful not to put anyone on the spot with this question. Ask for volunteers or begin with your own answer as a model of openness.

Question 7. Rebuke has to be used with great care. Rebuke in itself can crush a person's spirit or send him or her away feeling worthless or condemned. Our tone in rebuke has to be undergirded with genuine love. We might be inclined to say that rebuke should always be done in private, and certainly there are times when that approach is best, but Jesus seems to have rebuked James and John in front of the whole group. Maybe there were other disciples who needed to learn from Jesus' rebuke of these hot-headed brothers.

Question 8. In his wise and loving plan, God allowed one disciple to live (Peter) and another to die (James). Apart from Judas Iscariot's suicide, this is the only death of an apostle recorded in Scripture. The approximate date of James's execution is A.D. 44.

Study 5. Philip. John 6:1-13.

Purpose: To cultivate a deeper confidence in Jesus' power to work in life's impossible situations.

Question 1. The feeding of the five thousand is the only miracle of Jesus recorded in all four Gospels. It marked a significant turning point in Jesus' ministry—from the height of popularity to the point where many of his disciples were turning away from him (Jn 6:66).

The difficult aspects of this situation center around three issues: (1) the size of the crowd—Matthew says that the count of five thousand did not include women and children (Mt 14:21); (2) the remoteness of the area—there were no village or market towns nearby for the people to buy food; and (3) limited resources—the disciples did not have enough money to buy even a small amount of food for everyone, and the only food they could find was a boy's lunch.

Question 2. The crowds followed Jesus not to obey him but because of the miracles he had performed on those who were sick. That is not a bad motive for following Jesus, but it demonstrates that they may not have grasped the deeper spiritual demands of being one of Jesus' followers. After the miraculous meal, the crowd wanted to make Jesus king and follow him to Jerusalem to overthrow the Roman occupiers.

Question 3. Philip was the obvious person to ask first about how to solve this problem, since he came from the town of Bethsaida, the nearest town to them (Jn 1:44). Jesus already had a plan in mind, but he used the problem to test Philip's faith. Jesus wanted Philip to say, "I don't know how to solve this problem, Lord, but you do! What can I do to help?"

Question 4. Philip's response demonstrated that he is only thinking on the natural level, at the level of the marketplace. One denarius was a day's pay for a laborer; two hundred denarii (v. 7; see also Mk 6:37) represented eight month's wages. But the crowd was so large, even if they had that much money, it would only provide each person with a small piece of bread.

Question 5. Those of us who are like Philip try to figure out how God can solve our problems or how we can solve them with our abilities, our money and our efforts. We turn to God for help only when we've exhausted every other way.

Question 7. Philip must have been stunned by this miracle. Not only did everyone eat their fill (including the apostles), but large baskets of food were left over. (How many baskets? Twelve. How many disciples? Interesting!) Philip got a glimpse of God's abundant provision, just like we see the generosity of God's grace when he works in the difficult situations we face.

Question 8. Philip learned that day to trust Jesus. He also learned about God's goodness and what it means to be grateful to God. Philip learned too the futility of trying to solve problems that are beyond our control.

Question 9. Give your group members some time to respond to the final question. Perhaps you could pray for each situation as it is shared. Restrain the "Philips" in the group from giving their advice and suggestions about how to solve each problem.

Study 6. John. Matthew 20:20-28.

Purpose: To explore the concepts of leadership and success as they are expressed in Jesus' kingdom.

Question 1. The mother of James and John was not just their mother; she is also likely Jesus' aunt, named Salome (compare Mt 27:55-56 with Mk 15:40; see also Jn 19:25, where she is called Mary's sister). In the biblical world older women were given special respect, and they could make awkward requests that men could not.

Question 2. Salome was asking Jesus to give her sons the places of prominence and power in his kingdom. Jesus had already promised that the disciples would sit on twelve thrones (Mt 19:28), and she wanted to make sure that her sons would have the most important places. Later in his Gospel, Matthew uses the same phrase to refer to the thieves crucified with Jesus "one on his right side and one on his left" (Mt 27:38). The places of honor that James and John desired so strongly were given to two criminals.

In today's setting, Salome was asking that her sons have titles of authority next in rank only to Jesus—or lucrative spots on the corporate board or prominent recognition among spiritual leaders or places of high media coverage. Neither son would overshadow Jesus, of course; they just wanted to be next in line.

Question 3. In Mark's account of this incident, James and John come on their own to Jesus (Mk 10:35). Mark leaves Salome out in order to show where the responsibility for this request really lies. Even in Matthew's account, Jesus responds to Salome's request by speaking to the two brothers, not just to her (v. 22). The fact that the other disciples were upset with the two brothers (v. 24) demonstrates that the idea for this confrontation originated with them. Their mother was just a willing go-between.

Question 4. The "cup" is the cup of suffering that Jesus would soon drink. Jesus had just told his disciples that he would be betrayed, condemned, arrested and crucified (Mt 20:17-19). The cup Jesus would face was not the cup of glory and power, but the cup of pain and agony. The disciples were reluctant to believe that Jesus would suffer, but they weren't unaware of what Jesus believed was coming. The answer John and James gave to Jesus' question was not so much dishonest as clueless. It's the same false bravado that will lead Peter and the other apostles to say later that they will never disown or abandon Jesus, even when Jesus tells them pointedly that they will (Mt 26:33-35).

John and James would indeed share Jesus' cup. In Jewish thought, a "cup" was an experience or destiny. They think Jesus is talking about glory, but in reality he is talking about sorrow. Eventually James will be martyred (Acts 12:2) and John will be exiled to the prison island of Patmos (Rev 1:9-11). The other disciples are just as guilty of this race for greatness. They are indignant with James and John only because the brothers had thought of this tactic first! The debate over which of them would be greatest in the kingdom appears to have been a frequent topic among these twelve men (see Mt 18:1).

Question 5. The disciples had embraced a serious error about how things work in Jesus' kingdom. Jesus points out that the ways of the rulers of the "Gentiles" (used here in the sense of unbelievers) are not the ways of the kingdom. Those in places of authority in the world use threat and intimidation to get things done—they "lord it over" other people (still very true today!). The disciples thought the same principles would apply in the realm of Jesus' kingdom.

Question 6. Greatness in Christ's kingdom is the exact opposite of greatness in the secular world. Citizens of the kingdom are never to be marked by a lust for power over others. Instead greatness is attained through servanthood, as demonstrated by Jesus himself. The word *servant* in verse 26 is a translation of the Greek word *diakonos* (dee-a-cone-oss), meaning a household servant. It became the basic term in the early church for a minister or deacon—a leader marked by a willingness to serve. The idea is intensified in verse 27 by the use of the word *slave* (Greek: *doulos* [**due**-loss]). In the world "the greatest" and "the slave" are opposites; in the realm where Jesus reigns, they are the same.

Question 7. Jesus was God the Son, Israel's legitimate King, the promised Deliverer of his people. He could have demanded that his disciples spend their time and energy and resources meeting his needs. Instead Jesus poured out his life and time and resources meeting the needs of others. The world measures success in how much we get; Jesus measures it in how much we give away.

Questions 8-9. These questions hopefully will promote some serious soul-searching and prompt a deeper openness to the Holy Spirit. A person's attitude in describing how he or she serves others can tell you a lot. Bragging about it so that we get acclaim from others takes our actions out of the realm of servanthood and into the realm of using others to make ourselves look good.

Study 7. Thomas. John 20:19-29.

Purpose: To work through any issues of doubt about Jesus and to come to a new level of assurance and faith.

Introduction. Thomas is also mentioned in John 11:16, 14:1-6, and 21:2. Both the Hebrew root of the name Thomas and the Greek word *Didymus* mean "twin." Thomas's twin is never identified in Scripture.

Question 1. Jesus suddenly appeared in a room with locked doors. Just as Jesus' body had passed through the grave clothes at his resurrection (Jn 20:6-8), so it passed through the locked doors of the room and simply materialized in their presence. At the same time Jesus wants the disciples to know that he is real, not a dream or hallucination. So he speaks and he shows the wounds from his crucifixion. This was not some "spiritual" resurrection in the hearts and minds of the disciples; it was a bodily resurrection. Jesus' human body was raised in glory, never to die again.

Question 2. Jesus bestows his peace on men who had known nothing but turmoil and fear for three days. He then gives them a job to do, a new mission. They would no longer travel with Jesus or even as a band of men, but would go into their world with a message of grace. Jesus then grants them the power to carry out that mission by breathing out the Holy Spirit on them. This was a taste, a temporary empowerment that would become permanent in a few weeks on the day of Pentecost (Acts 2). Finally, Jesus gives his disciples the authority to pronounce sins forgiven. Only God can forgive sins, but once a person receives the gift of God's grace through faith in Jesus, they stand forgiven—and we can declare that to be true.

Question 3. When Thomas was told about what the other disciples had seen, he remained unconvinced. Thomas had to have proof that the person they claimed to have seen had a direct physical connection with the Jesus who was crucified. He wanted to see the wounds from the nails and the soldier's spear. He would not accept some sentimental memory of Jesus conjured up in the minds of the other disciples. This had to be the real thing or he would not believe.

Most scholars believe that those who were crucified were not nailed to the cross through the palms of their hands. The bone structure in the middle of the hand could not have supported a person's weight on the cross unless their arms were also tied to the cross. It's likely that Jesus was nailed to the cross through his wrists, between the two bones of the forearm. The word translated "hands" in verse 25 could be used to describe any part of the area of the hand or forearm.

Question 4. Jesus waited eight days before he appeared to all the disciples again. The disciples are still frightened and the doors are still locked, but Jesus again materializes among them. Jesus reveals to Thomas (and the others) that he hears their words even when he is not physically present. We are not told if Thomas actually touched the wounds of Jesus, but the impression given is that the sight and the sound of Jesus were enough to convince Thomas that this really was Jesus risen from the dead.

Perhaps the best approach to those who doubt the truth about Jesus is to leave them alone, rather than try to hammer them with arguments. God can still work in times of silence and reflection to open a person's heart and mind to faith and acceptance. Some credit should also go to Thomas for allowing himself to remain in the place where God could work best to bring him to faith. He didn't abandon the other disciples (leave the church) and cut himself off from their influence and help.

Question 5. Jesus is not angry with Thomas or condemning of his doubt. Instead he encourages Thomas's tiny faith: "Stop remaining in a state of unbelief and show yourself to be a believer" (v. 27).

Question 6. Thomas was so overcome with reverence and awe that he uttered one of the clearest confessions in the New Testament of Jesus' supremacy and deity. "The most unyielding skeptic has bequeathed to us the most profound confession" (D. A. Carson, *The Gospel of John* [Grand Rapids: Eerdmans, 1990], p. 659). Jesus accepts Thomas's confession without hesitation. If Jesus did not know that he was fully God in human form, he should have stopped Thomas and corrected his perspective. Instead Jesus received Thomas's worship without question or correction.

Question 7. Jesus commends Thomas for his belief in the face of irrefutable evidence, but then he promises to bless those who believe without actually seeing the risen Jesus. The word *blessed* carries the meaning of "accepted by God." Thomas, like all the witnesses of the resurrection, saw and believed; those of us who have believed since have relied on that eyewitness testimony, but we have believed without literal sight of the risen Jesus. The lack of sight does not mean, however, that our faith is less confident or joyful: "Though you have not seen him, you love him; . . . for you are receiving the end result of your faith, the salvation of your souls" (1 Pet 1:8-9). We who cannot share Thomas's experience of sight are blessed because we read or hear of his experience and come to share his faith.

Question 9. Jesus' "peace" is *shalom*—not just the absence of trouble or conflict, but a sense of unqualified well-being in every realm of life. Jesus had promised peace to the disciples before he went to the cross (Jn 14:27; 16:33), and now he fulfills that promise. True peace is given to those who are reconciled to God through the blood of the cross.

Study 8. Nathanael. John 1:43-51.

Purpose: To reaffirm our allegiance to Jesus as King and Lord, and to work on overcoming prejudice as we tell others about him.

Question 1. Each of the names and titles of Jesus has its own emphasis: "Jesus of Nazareth" points to his humanity and humble origins; "Rabbi" means teacher or leader; "Son of God" speaks to Jesus' deity and authority; "King of Israel" expresses Jesus' power and lordship; "Son of Man" is Jesus' favorite designation of himself. The prophet Daniel pictures the Son of Man as a heavenly being who receives authority over all nations from God (Dan 7:13-14).

Question 2. Although Philip does not use the term *Messiah* or *Christ* in this conversation, he certainly points to Jesus as the promised Deliverer. Both main sections of the Old Testament, the Law and the Prophets, describe an anointed One who would come to redeem God's people and restore to human beings what Adam had lost by his sin. Jesus is the fulfillment of these Old Testament promises (see also Jn 5:39).

Question 3. Just as Galileans were frequently looked down on by the more sophisticated Jews in Judea, it also appears that even fellow Galileans looked down on the residents of Nazareth. Nathanael was ready to dismiss Jesus simply because of what he presumed was the city of Jesus' origin. Philip responds with a challenge: "Come and see for yourself." Nazareth might be the despised city Nathanael thought it was, but there is an exception to every rule—and what an exception Jesus was! Philip's words are not only a challenge to Nathanael but an invitation to every reader of this Gospel: Investigate Jesus and his claims for yourself!

Question 5. The 2011 NIV translation gets Jesus' response right: "Here truly is an Israelite in whom there is no deceit" (v. 47). Jesus' point is that Nathanael was a man who was transparent in his motives and actions; he had no hidden agenda. Nathanael was willing to examine for himself the claims being made about Jesus even though he was at first skeptical.

Question 6. Nathanael realized that Jesus demonstrated supernatural knowledge about where he had been. Jesus "saw" Nathanael under the fig tree. Some interpreters have taken this to mean simply that as Jesus had come through the town he had noticed Nathanael sitting outside his home under the fig tree. Nathanael took Jesus' statement as meaning something very different. He took it that Jesus saw him from a distance, saw him with supernatural sight. Jesus' statement along with Philip's earlier declarations seem to have convinced Nathanael instantly of who Jesus was. Nathanael now respectfully addresses Jesus as "Rabbi" (v. 49), but then he goes far beyond what any student would say to his rabbi: "you are the Son of God; you are the king of Israel." Clearly, Nathanael was acknowledging Jesus as the promised Messiah and much more. In John's Gospel Nathanael is the first person who is said to believe.

Question 7. Depending on the composition of your group, you may want to ask for volunteers to answer this question. If you have those in the group who have not yet believed, they may be embarrassed if they are called on.

Question 8. Nathanael took a step of faith based largely on the miracle of Jesus' supernatural knowledge. Jesus promises that he will see even greater things, including the sign miracles promised in the Old Testament to accompany the Messiah's coming. In fact, Nathanael will see the greatness of the Son of Man that will far surpass even the heavenly vision of the patriarch Jacob (Gen 28:12). Jesus is telling Nathanael (and the other disciples) that they will receive heaven-sent confirmation that the one they have believed in as the Messiah is the One appointed and sent by God.

Question 9. As we grow in our relationship with Jesus, we develop a deeper understanding of who he is and how he works in our lives. Those insights usually come from Scripture, but our experience of walking through life with Christ and learning to trust him in every situation will also help us develop a deeper grasp of who he is and what he stands ready to do for those who follow him.

Study 9. Judas Iscariot. Matthew 26:14-30, 47-50; 27:1-10.

Purpose: To heed God's warning about turning away from Jesus and to see the tragic consequences of such betrayal.

Question 1. Judas clearly took the initiative to go to the religious leaders of Israel with the purpose of betraying Jesus for money. Judas was not tricked or made to think this was somehow in Jesus' best interests. Judas was motivated by greed. In John 12:6 we are told that Judas was the treasurer of the band of disciples and also that he stole from the group's money. Here Judas takes whatever the leaders offer and settles for what is a good amount of money, but not a lot. The silver coins were probably Jewish shekels, worth about four denarii each (a denarius was one day's wage for a hired worker). So Judas received less than half a year's wages to betray Jesus into the hands of those who wanted to kill him.

On the other side of the relationship, Jesus never singled Judas out for scorn or mistreatment. Even though he had known for some time that

Judas would be the betrayer, Jesus never treated Judas any differently than he treated the other disciples.

Question 2. Through the centuries, some scholars and interpreters have tried to explain or soften Judas's actions by saying that Judas was a misguided zealot who wanted to force Jesus to reveal himself as Israel's Messiah. *The Gospel of Judas*, a fourth-century Gnostic writing, says that Judas acted at Jesus' request so that Jesus could be offered as a sacrifice and fulfill his mission on earth. Some students of the Gospels think Judas really had no choice in the matter, but was predestined by God to be the betrayer. That view takes a very simplistic approach to God's sovereignty. Yes, God's plan included a betrayer. Even the amount of money paid to Judas was prophesied in the Old Testament Scriptures (Zech 11:12-13). But Judas made choices all along that moved him into that place as Jesus' betrayer. He was only outside the grace and forgiveness of Jesus because he refused to believe.

Judas at first gave every evidence of being a committed follower of Jesus. He preached with the other apostles and cast out evil spirits as the sign of the kingdom's soon arrival. But it seems that Judas quickly became disappointed with the pace of Jesus' mission. Then, when Jesus began to talk about his approaching arrest and death, Judas began to lose hope and confidence that Jesus really was the promised Messiah. Judas had hoped for a victorious Messiah who would bring in a golden age of prosperity for Israel. Now those hopes began to fade. On his side, Jesus may have begun to see evidences of Judas's declining interest—less attention to Jesus' teaching and more of a demand for access to money. Jesus probably began to notice Judas's theft from the group's resources.

Question 3. Judas took the tenderest expression of affection, a kiss, and made it a sign of betrayal. It would be like using a friendly offer of a cup of coffee to poison a neighbor! It was customary in Jesus' day for students to kiss their rabbi on the cheek or the hand, but Judas, appearing to act lovingly toward Jesus, made it a sign of treachery. Because the crowd came to get Jesus at night, they wanted to make sure they arrested the right man.

Question 5. It's possible to feel sorrow because we have been caught or exposed in wrongdoing, or because our actions resulted in consequences we had not considered. Some interpreters of Matthew believe that Judas genuinely repented. The evidence of that repentance is his confession of the sin and the return of the money. Other interpreters (myself included) do not see this as genuine repentance. Judas did admit his sin, but not to God or to Jesus. He returned the money out of guilt. The deciding factor for me is that Judas's remorse did not produce the fruit of repentance in his life. Rather than going back to Jesus for forgiveness, Judas committed suicide.

Question 6. Jesus had continually and repeatedly held out a hand of grace to Judas. He would have cleansed and forgiven Judas and even restored him to a place of ministry (as he did to Peter after the disciple's denial of Jesus). The first drops of blood shed by Jesus on the cross would have been for Judas.

Question 7. The important factor in your response is to take the person's concern seriously. Don't just casually blow it off. Point the person to Jesus' clear promises to forgive those who come in faith and confession to him (for example, 1 Jn 1:9; 2:1-2, 12).

Question 8. This question needs to be handled with discernment, but it is a significant part of any discussion about Judas. Carefully avoid any blanket statements about suicide, such as, "all those who commit suicide are lost." God is the judge of our hearts. Even the apostle Paul admitted being so discouraged that he "despaired of life itself" (2 Cor 1:8). Suicide is obviously never a choice that God desires or blesses, but we need to be very careful in the judgments we pass on those caught up in it.

Question 9. Judas's spiritual slide away from Jesus did not come suddenly. He became careless with his life and opened his mind more and more to Satan's influence. Judas began to tolerate sinful behavior and resentment in his life. He thought his way was best in spite of what Jesus thought or said. Judas began to spend time with Jesus' enemies. All or any of those steps can lead us into the same spiritual decline from the Lord. The person who thinks he or she would never betray Jesus like Judas did has already been deceived by spiritual pride and is a prime target for the enemy! "Every follower of Jesus should reflect on his or her capacity to imitate the monstrous treachery of Judas" (David Turner, *Matthew*, Baker Exegetical Commentary on the New Testament [Grand Rapids: Baker, 2008], p. 621).

Now or Later. As a leader, you may want to give this issue some thought because it will most likely arise in your discussion of Judas. You may want to be prepared to explain both views of Judas and salvation. You may also want to give your position on the matter. Your pastor can give you some direction on this issue as well. Don't expect to "solve" the problem to everyone's satisfaction. It's been debated for 2000 years!

Study 10. Three Others. Luke 18:18-30.

Purpose: To understand that some believers serve Jesus in obscurity, but they have eternal rewards from the Lord.

Question 1. Our natural tendency is to pay attention to someone with wealth and to try to get them interested and committed to our work. While we are busy trying to pull people in, Jesus often tells people to go home until they are ready to make a commitment to him. Or, like in the case of this rich man, Jesus begins throwing roadblocks in their way in order to expose their true motives. This man is called a ruler, but we cannot tell if he is a religious ruler or a civil ruler.

Question 2. The ruler addresses Jesus as "good teacher." Only rarely in Jewish literature or custom was a rabbi called "good." Jesus responds by saying, "No one is good—except God alone." Perhaps Jesus was trying to get the man to realize that Jesus was more than a rabbi; he was God himself. The heart of the ruler's question is this: "What must I *do* to inherit eternal life?" (v. 18). The man obviously thought that eternal life was earned by doing something—keeping the commandments, going to church, doing religious things. Jesus seems at first to agree! He implies that the ruler should keep the commandments. Jesus quotes commandments from the second tablet of the law, the later commandments that have to do with loving other people. The ruler claims that he has kept those commandments since his youth, since the day around his thirteenth birthday when he formally took upon himself the obligation to keep the law.

Question 3. Jesus, however, points out the one thing the man lacked by asking him to sell all his possessions and distribute them to the poor. The one thing the ruler lacked was, in fact, an all-encompassing issue in his life. Jesus wanted this man to stop trusting in his wealth (his "god"). If he gave all his wealth away, the only thing left to trust for eternal life was Jesus. Then (and only then) would the man be ready to follow the

Lord. The ruler discovers sadly that for him, life's first priority is not God's kingdom but his own riches. Jesus will always require from us the single earthly security that we are most tempted to lean on. Only then are we ready to follow Jesus with a whole heart.

Question 5. It's hard for a rich person to enter God's kingdom because the rich are tempted to trust their money, not God. Wealth can certainly smooth out a lot of life's trials, but eternal life comes only by faith, by trusting in Jesus alone. Jesus' statement does not mean, of course, that rich people *can't* be saved. God is able to draw them to genuine faith by his power and grace.

Question 6. Peter and the other disciples may have felt somewhat unrewarded for the sacrifices they had made to follow Jesus. Many of them left thriving businesses and the security of home and friends to join themselves to Jesus. Family ties were not ignored, but were ranked under their first loyalty to Jesus. These men had linked their reputations and their futures to Jesus and, at times, they struggled with the personal cost of their loyalty to him. Down through the centuries of the church, multitudes of disciples have left behind privilege and wealth and family and comfort to follow Jesus. The Lord may not call us to leave everything to follow him, but that spirit of willing obedience should mark each of us as disciples.

Question 7. Jesus promises recompense for any sacrifice we make for the kingdom of God. In this age, he will bring other believers to us who will act as parents or children or siblings to replace those left behind to be obedient to Jesus' call. Christians should look for those opportunities not just to have our needs met but also to be used to bless others who have sacrificed the joys and comforts of life and family to serve Jesus. The blessings of this age will be carried over into eternity as we experience the joys of those relationships forever.

Question 8. The Lord may be asking someone in the group to serve him in a way that requires the sacrifice of security or a career path or closeness to family. Encourage that person to be sure it is the Lord's voice they hear. Remind them of Jesus' promises to restore to them "many times" whatever they leave behind to serve him. There are smaller sacrifices all of us can make to serve Christ more effectively—sacrifices of time, energy, resources, comfort or hobbies. Jesus watches how willing we are to give things over to him when he asks.